THE · BOOK · OF
HORSES

BY · GLENN · BALCH

SCHOLASTIC BOOK SERVICES
New York Toronto London Auckland Sydney Tokyo

Front cover: Colour Library International
Back cover: Walter Chandoha

ISBN 0-590-32733-X

12 11 10 9 8 7 6 5 4 3 2 1   9   2 3 4 5 6/8

Printed in the U.S.A.   21

CONTENTS

MEET THE HORSE

VAN DER MEID-MONKMEYER

A HORSE is a beautiful and graceful animal, and when you meet him you'll see how wonderfully friendly he is too. Unless you have ridden a horse, you can't imagine how exciting the whole world seems when you are high up on his sturdy back. No words can really show you the thrill of a gallop, when the wind whips through the horse's long mane and you feel the power of his strong muscles beneath you, carrying you across a countryside that seems to race past you.

Have you ever looked into a horse's big dark eyes or stroked his satiny coat? Have you ever offered a horse a lump of sugar and seen how gently he takes it off your palm? If you have ever done any of these things, you know that the horse is your friend.

Some Horse History

Nowadays, we don't see horses as often as we once did, but for thousands and thousands of years — until very recently — the horse was man's greatest helper and most useful friend.

How do we know? We have found pictures on cave walls — some of them at least 50,000 years old — that show man and horse working together in all kinds of jobs. From these pictures, and from later written records, we can tell that wherever man went, his loyal horse went too. Some of these records tell us that horses lived in the same tents as their masters. Some were even buried in the same graves.

If you had lived just a hundred years ago, you would have met and perhaps owned a horse soon after you were born. You would have ridden or driven him to school, to church — just about everywhere you went. If you had been an Indian boy or girl, you would have been tied onto a horse's back almost before you could walk.

Did you know that the very first horses lived right here in America? We know this because bones of these ancient horses have been found in Wyoming and New Mexico. By studying these bones, scientists are able to tell us what these prehistoric horses looked like. They were just about the size of jack rabbits! And they had three horny toes on each foot.

You might find this hard to believe when you compare the tiny creature with his modern descendant. Our horses today are tall and muscular, with sturdy hoofs instead of toes. They are among the fastest of all animals. Their great speed and stamina enable them to run away from danger.

Even though the horse was born in America, he emigrated to other parts of the world, where he grew into the horse we know today. But how did he get back to this country? The first modern horse was brought here by Christopher Columbus. In fact, all of the horses in America today are descendants of those brought here by Columbus and the explorers who followed him. Isn't it exciting to think that a horse you've seen may be descended from one that came here on the *Pinta*, the *Niña*, or the *Santa Maria*?

Lippizan horses of the Spanish Riding School. Horses like these were first brought to America by the Spanish explorers.

BORSIG-MONKMEYER

MAN'S MOST USEFUL FRIEND

YOU'VE probably heard that the dog is man's best friend. Even if true, the horse has certainly been his most useful friend. For almost as far back as the beginning of time, horses have carried men from one place to another on their strong backs. They have pulled plows and wagons and buggies and stagecoaches.

Horses for Hunting

With the horse's help, men could chase and kill large, swift-moving animals for meat to feed their families. They could obtain more animal products, such as hides for tents and fur robes and clothes for warmth during cold weather. It was only after they had learned to use the horse that the Indians could hunt the great buffalo herds.

The beauty and power of horses thundering across a field.

But before men could use the horse's strength to help them, they first had to catch him. This was not at all easy to do, for the first horses were very wild animals, and the men were on foot.

You might try to guess how the first horse was caught. Perhaps some children saw a foal or a colt whose mother had been killed, and decided that the lonely, long-legged animal would make a fine pet. After they had taken the orphan back to their cave or tent and fed him for a while, they realized how loving a well-cared-for horse can be.

Horses for Riding

Our ancestors soon realized that if they were to use the horse's strength, they would have to find a way to control him. And so they invented the bridle. Of course, the first bridle didn't look like the ones we have today, but it did allow the rider to guide and stop his horse.

Mare and colts enjoy good grazing on a Maryland farm.

GRETE MANNHEIM

The first saddles were made by tying skins and robes to the horse's back. Today this type of saddle is called a packsaddle. It is still used in very mountainous country where there are no roads for cars and trucks.

The riding saddle was probably invented much later than the packsaddle. The first riding saddle was probably only a piece of animal skin. Some bright man realized that the skins could be made much softer by stuffing them with grass. He found that these stuffed skins could be held in place with straps that went around the horse, and that was the first girth, or cinch.

When dangling made his legs tired, man made foot rests from forked tree limbs and leather straps, and hung them from both sides of the saddles. These crude footrests were the first primitive stirrups.

Horses for Hauling

Another important discovery was made when men learned that horses could drag more than they could carry. With a new type of harness, horses were hitched to sleds made of limbs and twigs. This greatly increased their usefulness.

But there was a much better way to use the horse's strength for hauling loads than by just having him drag them across the ground. This was by building carts and wagons. Before man could make a wagon, however, he had to discover the wheel. This looks like a simple invention to us, because today almost every conveyance moves on wheels — the bicycle, car, train, and even airplane. When we roller-skate, we are carrying ourselves on wheels.

But you can see that the discovery of the wheel was not as easy as might appear when you realize that the Indians did not use it until they learned about it from the white man.

After the wheel was put into use, people learned that the horse could supply power for it. First, horses were used to pull crude wagons and carts. Chariots, such as those described in the Bible, were used by warriors. But the horse could do many other things besides hauling people and goods. He could turn wheels that crushed rocks and ground grain. By the use of ropes and small wheels called pulleys, his great strength could be harnessed to raise logs and beams into the air, to help in building houses. In all these ways the horse was acting as an engine, or motor. That is why today we still talk about the "horsepower" of our cars.

As men began to use the horse more and more, their whole way of life changed. A farmer could grow more crops, because he had a horse to plow his fields. The horse could also haul his crops to the village or the town. This meant that the people in the town didn't have to worry about growing their own food.

Naturally, everyone wanted a horse. And the wealthier a man was, the more horses he had. Some men went into the business of raising and training horses, so that there would be plenty of them for all the jobs that had to be performed. Everywhere you went, you saw horses, just as we see cars and machines today. If you yourself had lived then, you wouldn't have had to learn about horses. You would have grown up with them.

THE RIGHT HORSE
FOR THE JOB

MAN had not been using horses for long before he discovered that there are differences between them. Some were good at one job, some at another. The smaller, slim horses were faster and more graceful. They were best for riding and hunting. The larger, sturdier horses were ideal for hauling heavy loads and carrying bigger burdens.

People soon realized that the best way to get work done by horses was simply to choose the right horse for the particular job. From this, it was only a step to the idea of developing special kinds of horses. This was the beginning of what we call "breeding," which has since given us Thoroughbreds, Morgans, Standardbreds, and all the other kinds that we know today. The various breeds of dogs and cattle came about in the same way.

The "Great Horse"

In Europe, during the Middle Ages, horses were needed for battle. They carried the heavily armored knights, and this meant that they had to be big and powerful. Speed was less important. The horse that was developed for this purpose was so large, in fact, that it was known as the "Great Horse." And because knights rode these horses, the people liked them too.

But not everybody was a knight. Horses were also in great demand for hauling and for plowing the fields. They weren't so important for traveling, because many people never went more than a mile or two from their native village. Since farming and transporting goods were necessary, however, men began developing horses to do these jobs. They had to be big and strong, but they didn't have to be as huge as the knights' horses.

Work Horses

Today, even though the work horse has largely been replaced by machines, we still have special breeds of heavy horses. Sometimes you will see them pulling large wagons. The best-known breeds of these horses, which are called draft horses, are the Percherons, the Clydesdales, the Shires, and the Belgians. Some of them weigh more than a ton.

Our American frontier was a very different place from the Europe of several hundred years ago. We didn't need a horse that could carry a knight in heavy clanking armor. Since the settlements were far apart, we needed horses that could cover long distances. Sometimes a man and his

Percherons like this powerful horse once carried knights to the Crusades. Originally from Normandy, France, Percherons are now bred in America for farm and draft horses.

14

horse were away from home for a whole year. They had to travel through rough country — over unknown hills, across hot, dusty plains, through strange forests. And they always had to be on guard against unfriendly Indians.

This was not a job for the heavy horses of Europe. Heavy horses couldn't outrun the fleet Indian ponies. If they had been used to pull stagecoaches, they would have lumbered along like work horses. They would have been useless on narrow, winding trails and in dense forests. And there was something else wrong with them: they ate too much. We needed a horse that could live off the country.

We needed a fast horse to cover the great distances. A sure-footed horse for trail riding. A courageous horse to swim the wide rivers and climb the steep mountains. The wild horses were ideal, because they lived in this kind of country. But they were hard to catch and hard to train. And so we developed a light, strong horse, and this horse did the job. To him we owe, in large part, the development of the West.

Not so many years ago, these horses were used for all kinds of work — and there was plenty of work for large, sturdy horses to do. What would you think if you heard a fire alarm and then saw horses speeding down the street, hauling a bright red fire engine with smoke pouring from it? This was a common sight fifty years ago, and the powerful "fire horses" were popular with everybody. Horses did something else that might surprise you, too. They pulled boats and barges through canals by walking along a path beside the water.

When America was being settled, and the frontier was

moving westward, horses helped our forefathers build their homes in the wilderness. Whole forests had to be turned into farms, and this meant that there was a great deal of heavy work to be done. All this shows that the "work horse" really earned his name.

Horses for the West

In those frontier days, almost everybody worked with horses. Everybody used them for traveling, and many people raised or trained them. Every village had its blacksmith's shop, with its roaring fire and huge anvil. And the veterinarian or horse doctor was a very important man, because he treated horses when they were sick.

Since horses were so important, you can imagine how necessary it was for people to know how to handle them. A man who could ride well and understood horses was a valuable worker. The women in the frontier country became good riders too, and the children grew up with horses. Horsemanship was just about the first thing they learned.

Pair in work harness pulling a light plow. Much work on small eastern farms is done by lighter horses like these.

GRETE MANNHEIM

SOME FAVORITE RIDING HORSES

AS a means of speedy travel, the horse is hopelessly outmoded. The jeep can run circles around him — except in one place. In rugged back country and on steep mountain trails the horse is still the best means of transportation known to man. The horse (and this includes the mule) can make his way over the roughest going and carry a rider or a pack at the same time.

But the real future of the horse in America lies in the pleasure he can give to people like the readers of this book. That future is brighter than you might think. And it is getting still brighter as new and faster work methods result in more spare time for everyone, more time to do what one pleases. It pleases a lot of people to own, raise, and ride horses.

Why is this? With some, it is because they like horses. They admire the horse's beauty and willingness, his ability to learn to do a number of things. They like the horse's friendliness. They get pleasure from training horses and working with them.

Others are finding that horses can become a profitable hobby or business. They own, raise, and train horses to supply the demand of people who ride for pleasure and recreation.

The growing interest in horses for pleasure has had a good influence on the people who breed and train them. There are more and better breeding associations than ever before. There are more fine saddle horses today than when horses were necessary for transportation.

Thousands of saddle clubs have been organized by pleasure riders. There are many mounted sheriff's posses and fancy drill teams. Horse shows are held from coast to coast. Some of the biggest are staged at Madison Square Garden in New York and the Cow Palace in San Francisco. Fine horses are bringing the highest prices in history.

Arabians and Thoroughbreds

The blood of the proud Arabian was important in the development of all light-horse breeds. The Bedouins so loved their horses that they shared their tents with them. An Arabian was the wonder horse of the desert, superb in intelligence, stamina, loyalty, and beauty. He is still admired for these excellent qualities and has won an enthusiastic following in the United States. Arabians are noted for their gentleness, good disposition, and dependability, especially as mounts for pleasure riding and trail riding.

Horses that were developed for racing are Thoroughbreds. Before the train and the automobile were invented,

Gray Arabian: "Arabians are noted for their gentleness, good disposition, and dependability."

the horse was the swiftest means of travel. He was therefore prized for his speed, which became the supreme objective of Thoroughbred breeding. Today millions of people go to the race tracks every year to watch Thoroughbreds compete against other Thoroughbreds in both long- and short-distance racing.

The Thoroughbred was produced by crossing the so-called "hot" blood of Arabian and Barb stallions with the "cold-blooded" English mares. The result was the speediest horses the world has ever known, and they have since dominated flat racing (on a level track) as well as the steeplechase (a course with obstacles to be jumped). Because of the popularity of racing, interest in the Thoroughbred is high, and horsemen are constantly trying to improve the breed.

Standardbreds

The Standardbreds, developed for buggy use, are the speedsters of the harness tracks. Few sights are more thrilling than a field of either trotters or pacers sweeping down the course.

Many people, however, are interested in horses for pleasure rather than speed. These are the horsemen who want to take part in all kinds of riding sports. For this they need "doing" horses, able to perform the particular job required. This has resulted in still more specialized breeding.

Saddlebreds

If you like a stylish, high-stepping horse, the answer is an American Saddlebred, which was developed in this country. The Saddlebred is a strong-bodied horse with proud carriage and vigorous, spirited action. He is a pleasure to ride and to watch.

American Saddlebred, five-gaited.

Morgan: Junior Champion Stallion "Orcland Dondarling."

The three- and five-gaited horses of the show ring come from Saddlebred stock. Many others of this breed are used for pleasure and trail riding.

Tennessee Walkers

Another specialized horse is the Tennessee Walker, bred for use by the overseers on the large southern plantations. He is noted for the comfort and speed of his running walk, a motion that is said to be like sitting in a rocking chair. The Tennessee Walker is a first-class pleasure horse and has an enthusiastic following as a show-ring performer.

Morgans

One of the most unusual developments in light-horse breeding is the Morgan. The Morgan can be traced back to a single stallion who didn't even have a name and was called after his owner, Justin Morgan. This small but powerful stallion demonstrated marked ability in several fields, winning both pulling and racing contests, sometimes in a single afternoon. Even more remarkable was the fact that this horse was able to pass on his excellent qualities to his colts. The blood of the little stallion today flows in fine, handsome pleasure horses in every state.

Quarter Horses

Another American breed of increasing interest to all riders is the Quarter Horse. This animal is famed for his short-distance speed, his lightning-fast reactions, and a sixth sense that is known as "cow savvy." His admirers claim that the Quarter Horse is the ablest of working horses. And today's top calf roping and bulldogging horses are almost without exception of Quarter Horse breeding. The powerful hindquarters enable this horse to get away in a flash. With his compact body, short legs, and sturdy muscles, he can make sharp turns and stop quickly—an ability especially prized when an animal has to be cut out of a herd.

The Quarter Horse is also outstanding for racing short distances—a talent that gave him his name. In Colonial

Western Quarter Horse (colt): "the best of short-distance racers, and a top working mount for anybody's corral."

Appaloosa crossing a barrier in a Trail Horse class: one of the tests in western horse shows.

days the most convenient tracks were the main streets in towns, usually about a quarter of a mile long. Such a distance requires fast starting, and for this the Quarter Horse has been without equal. Today, Quarter Horses are being bred with Thoroughbreds to produce a more slender horse with speed over greater distances. They are very popular mounts with English-style riders.

Appaloosas

The so-called color horses are gaining in popularity among the light breeds. These are the palomino, the pinto, the albino, and the Appaloosa. The Appaloosa has an especially interesting history, having been bred by the Nez Percé Indians in the Northwest long before the famous Lewis and Clark expedition. These spotted horses were noted for their gentleness and easy gait.

Jumpers

Many phases of riding are dominated by horses of a certain breed. But not the spectacular sport of jumping. The jumper can be of mixed breeding, and is often a Thoroughbred. In general, the typical jumper is just a big, rangy horse with a long, elastic stride and powerful hindquarters to supply the drive necessary to get the horse and rider "up and over."

Though they are the result of specialized breeding programs, the majority of light horses in the United States are not specialists. They are the mounts of the pleasure rider, the horses of saddle clubs, and drill teams. Through their obedience, willingness, loyalty, adaptability, and general excellence they earn their oats and the affectionate regard of their masters.

Part-blooded mare and her filly: the mare is of Arab and Morgan type; the filly's sire was a Saddlebred.

Western style: ranch horse and cowboy ready for work.

RIDING STYLES

VAN DER MEID-MONKMEYER

ARE you going to ride English style or western style? What you decide will make a big difference in the clothes and equipment you buy.

The Western Style

If you choose western, you must have a pair of high-heeled boots with wrinkled toes; a fancy design will be stamped into the leather. You will wear tight-fitting blue jeans. You should have a wide leather belt with a silver buckle showing a man on a bucking horse. The shirt will be bright-colored, with pearl snaps instead of buttons.

Traditionally, the Western rider's hat is of felt—pearl-gray, black, brown, purple, maroon, or orange. You will also need fringed chaps (loose leather overalls), and silver spurs with rowels like silver dollars.

The front of your saddle will have a pommel with a big round horn, and there will be a high cantle to support your back. The wooden stirrups will be wide-bottomed for quick dismounting, and their "fenders" will be of heavy

English style: A properly turned out horse and rider for showing.

leather to protect you from horse sweat. If you expect to ride in thorny brush, it will be well to use covered stirrups for extra protection.

The saddle will be anchored to your horse with two stout leather girths or cinches. With the addition of a lariat and a saddle blanket, your rig will weigh about thirty-five pounds.

The straps of the bridle will have silver trimmings; there will be a long-shanked curb bit. The single reins will be good and strong.

With a slicker roll containing lunch and a thermos behind the cantle, you are ready for whatever comes during a long day's ride in rough country. If you want to rest or take a nap, you can stake out your horse with the lariat and use the saddle blanket to lie on. It's quite comfortable.

The English Style

English equipment is quite different. The English riding habit includes trim breeches that fit snugly inside the tops of high boots, or jodhpurs—pants made of stretch material held tight to the ankle by an elastic strap under the instep. With jodhpurs go paddock boots (ankle-high laced shoes) or a high shoe with an elasticized ankle. Your tailored jacket will be tweed or a solid dark color, flared below the waist. You will also wear a stock or neck scarf, closely tied, and a hunt cap, hard to protect your head.

The English saddle is very light, but well made and fully equal to its purpose. Comfort is the keynote of the flat saddle. It has no horn, and a very low cantle.

The stirrup leathers are narrow and flexible, and the stirrups are made of lightweight steel. There is a single girth, which may be leather or canvas. Some riders favor canvas because it is washable. The girth is attached to the saddle by straps and buckles on both sides, so that it may be taken off for cleaning.

An English bridle usually has a snaffle bit, or a curb bit with double reins. The reins are closed at the ends, one set by a buckle and the other sewn together. The curb bit is used when you need more control.

Thoroughbred Hunter: mixed Arab and English breeding has produced the speediest horses for racing and the steeple-chase.

Typical western mount showing western tack or gear.

Now you are ready for the park, the bridle path, or the tanbark ring, whichever you choose.

But what about the horses for riding English or western style? Oh yes, the horses... Well, Westerners are inclined to favor showy colors, like the golden palomino, or the striking color combinations of the pinto and the Appaloosa. English-style riders have shown a preference for the solid shades—black, bay, brown, and chestnut. The Westerner likes ruggedness and sure-footedness; the English-style rider pays more attention to fine appearance and smooth gait.

RAY SKOBE-DE WYS

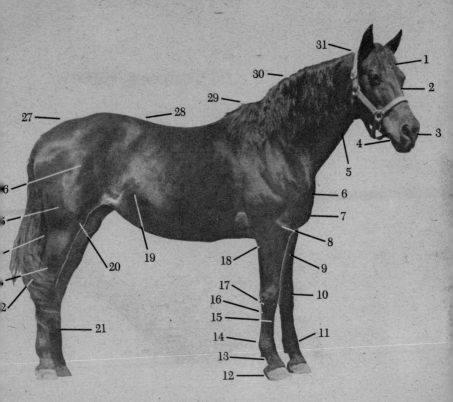

The Horse

1. FOREHEAD
2. FACE
3. MUZZLE
4. JAW
5. WINDPIPE
6. POINT OF SHOULDER
7. BREAST, BRISKET, CHEST
8. ARM
9. FOREARM
10. KNEE
11. FETLOCK JOINT, ANKLE
12. HOOF
13. PASTERN
14. FETLOCK
15. CANNON BONE
16. TENDON
17. CHESTNUT
18. ELBOW
19. FLANK
20. STIFLE
21. CANNON
22. HOCK
23. SECOND THIGH, GASKIN
24. QUARTER
25. THIGH
26. HIP JOINT
27. CROUP
28. LOINS
29. WITHERS
30. CREST
31. POLL

THE PROUD MUSTANGS

WUNDER-MONKMEYER

ONE of the most thrilling sights for a horse lover is a proud mustang, head held high, against a western skyline. He symbolizes a bold defiance, an independence and a love of freedom that are all too rapidly becoming things of the past.

Wild horses have always been a favorite subject for writers. The mares are sturdy. The stallions are crafty and strong. But in America these mustangs are not and never have been wild in the true sense. They are descended from domestic horses.

This is a bit confusing, especially when some hard-bitten old horse herder tells you that mustangs are wilder than deer. In one way he is right. Wild horses will run at the approach of man; deer are far less easily disturbed.

Tame and Wild

Fear and caution are so strong in the wild horse that he resists all advances by man. He may have been caught and branded, yet still be "wild." It is well known that trained saddle horses which have broken out of their corrals are frequently the wildest of all, in the sense of being hard to catch.

In range country, the brand mark of the ranch is what distinguishes the tame horses from the wild ones. It is assumed that a "slick" (unbranded) horse is wild and that a branded one is owned. So the range rider finds it more accurate to use the terms "slick" and "branded," rather than "wild" and "tame," for the tame one may be much the "spookier" (more easily scared) of the two.

Wild horses once roamed the central and southwestern plains in herds numbering in the thousands. They were the descendants of horses that had escaped from the early explorers — mainly the Spanish Conquistadors. Unmolested, and with abundant grass to graze on, the herds increased with amazing rapidity. In some areas it was once possible to travel for an entire day without ever losing sight of huge bands of wild horses.

It seemed that wild horses, like the buffalo, could never die out. Anyone who could catch them was welcome to them. For many years the herds were a main source of supply for the Indians, who were always in need of horses. Sometimes they found it simpler and easier to steal tame animals from other Indians, or from the white settlements.

Wild ponies on Sable Island, Nova Scotia. Herds of wild horses and ponies still roam free in many parts of the world.

Capturing Wild Horses

Many methods of capturing wild horses were used, and men lay awake nights trying to devise others. Most methods involved running or trapping, or both. Patience and planning and time were required, plus tough saddle horses, for the wild ones had the advantage. They knew the country, and they were carrying no weight. Also, they had unbelievable determination and endurance.

Thousands were caught, trail-broken, and driven to the big horse markets. They were small but wonderfully strong and wiry. Some of the best saddle and buggy horses of the day came from the wild herds. No beast *really* wild could have been gentled in such numbers.

Wild ponies being driven across the inlet at Chincoteague Island, Virginia, for the annual pony-penning.

This great abundance couldn't last. It was not the catchers, however, that ended it; it was the settlers and barbed wire. The vast plains were fenced and turned to farming, robbing the wild horses of their home. The remnants of the herds were pushed back and back, into rougher, more desolate country. Here they made a gallant stand, but the forces against them were unrelenting and clever.

Wild Herds Today

It is only in those isolated, broken lands of sparse vegetation that the wild horse is still found. Perhaps the largest remaining wild-horse range is the place where the states of Idaho, Oregon, and Nevada come together. This is a wide, rugged area drained by the winding Owyhee River and its tributaries. Here in the steep-walled canyons the mustangs find food and refuge.

The Federal Bureau of Land Management is increasing grazing restrictions on government-owned ranges. To make the squeeze still tighter, canners and processors of animal foods pay a cash reward for any horse, wild or tame, young or old. So catching horses has become a profitable business.

Now the last strongholds of the wild horse are being invaded, not only by men on horses, but by jeeps and trucks and airplanes. Goggled aviators spook the herds down from the high ridges and out of the hidden canyons. Trucks and mounted men take up the chase in the flats.

What the settler and his barbed wire started, the catcher with his airplanes and jeeps is out to finish.

But the horse lover can find comfort in one thing. As long as any rugged, hard-to-reach back country remains, and as long as the ranchers turn their saddle stock and brood mares out onto the range, there will be wild horses — bands of mares led by proud stallions.

ON THE
DUDE RANCH

THE lanky, sun-tanned fellow squints down at you and drawls. "You been ridin' much lately?"

He's the wrangler. "Wrangling" is the old term for horse herding. This man is called a "dude wrangler" because he works on a dude ranch. A dude ranch invites paying guests to come and enjoy the activities and the scenery; it's a kind of ranch hotel.

Naturally, the people who enjoy dude ranches like the outdoors, and just as naturally a lot of the dude-ranch activity requires horses. The horses, therefore, are important to the ranch's success and are carefully chosen for the jobs to be done.

Horses for "dudes" running into the corral at Holzwarth Ranch near Grand Lake, Colorado.

The number one job is to carry the dudes safely where they wish to go. "I'll catch that buckskin for you," the wrangler says. "He's one of our best horses."

That means the man has sized up your riding ability, and Buck is the answer. It could have been Blue or Bell or Bonito.

You may feel that you can handle that spirited pinto over in the corner. But the wrangler is not convinced. He is planning a ride up the side of the mountain for you and your friends, and he wants to get you there and back in one piece.

Buck is a dude horse. There is no such thing as a fool-proof horse, but Buck is close to it. He is old enough to have done and seen most of the things that can happen on a ride, and he is sure-footed for the mountain trails. He knows exactly what he has to do, and he takes his time doing it. Just leave it to Buck. He will get you there and back safely.

Some guests are inclined to overestimate their riding ability. This has made the wrangler cautious. But if you show you can ride the first time out, he might saddle the pinto for you next time. He might even let you ride his own private horse, which you can be sure is one of the best.

Ranch Horses

The ranch has some young horses, being broken to saddle and trained so that they became part of the dude string later. They look lively and exciting, but they aren't safe to ride for a while yet. If they were dependable, they wouldn't be in the group still being trained.

Mountain trails are an exciting feature of riding in the West.

The big, heavy horses and the mules in the corral are not for riding. They are the pack animals. When you go on that five-day trip to the high lakes, these horses will carry the tents and the bedrolls and the pancake mix. They know how to edge around a tree and how to cat-foot along a narrow shelf without scrambling the eggs or smashing the expensive fishing rods and cameras in their packs. Good pack horses can add much to the success and pleasure of an outing.

It is the business of the dude ranch to see that you and the other guests have plenty of opportunity for fun and entertainment. You are encouraged to do the things you like best. If this happens to be fishing, you will be shown the best trout holes. If you are a camera fan, you will be taken to the most striking views. Picnics are held on the shores of the lake. Nimble-footed horses carry you on moonlight rides through the forest.

The ranch is also an operating cow outfit, so you can take part in the roundups. You can help with the branding. If you have the ability, you can try your hand at calf roping. The activity in the corrals is an entertainment feature.

Branding a steer on the open range. These spirited horses are Appaloosas.

Old Pete, the Bucker

On a lazy afternoon, one of the wranglers may say, "I feel pretty lucky today. Reckon I'll go down and try Old Pete."

Old Pete is a member of the dude-ranch string you haven't met yet. He and two or three more like him are not meant to be ridden. They are confirmed buckers, kept for just such an occasion as this.

You will hear about the wrangler's intention to ride Old Pete. The word always gets around, and in less time than it takes to tell, everybody who can get away is headed for the corrals.

Here you have the world's best rodeo seat, the top rail. A good rider or two from a neighboring ranch has happened by just in time to take part in the fun. The other buckers will be ridden, too.

These are different from the regular rodeos. Here everything takes place right before your eyes. There are no chutes for saddling, no walls nor flags nor banners to hide the view.

Fire is shining in Old Pete's eyes when the cowboys lead him in. He knows the game from past experience, and he is ready to do his part. One of the boys is on a "snubbin' horse," to assist in the saddling by holding Old Pete close. The others pull his head down and put a blindfold over his eyes. When he can't see, Old Pete's hind feet are not so accurate.

You can hear and smell the excitement as well as see it. The corral dust boils up. The cowboys dodge Old Pete's

"He arches his back and goes straight up in the air, bent like a hairpin."

hoofs. The scarred old bucking saddle is put in place, and the saddler cautiously fishes with a stick under Old Pete's belly for the cinch. He gets it, puts the strap through the ring and pulls it up, gently at first. You see the tremor run through Old Pete's sturdy frame, and you know he is just biding his time.

The cowboy heaves against the cinch, pulling it tight. He makes a firm tie, then steps back and says, "He's all yours," to the wrangler who felt lucky.

You wonder then if he is going to back out. There is something mighty wicked about the way Old Pete crouches. For a minute it looks as if the wrangler might. But then he rises, hitches up his pants, and throws his cigarette in the dust. He goes to Old Pete and, while the horse is still blindfolded and snubbed tight, eases himself into the saddle.

His lips twist in a bleak little smile as he measures the length he wants on the bucking rein. He pulls his hat down tight, nods to the snubbing-horse rider, and says, "Let's go."

Then things begin to happen! If you're one of the watching guests, hang on tight, so that you don't fall off the rail. The snubber turns Old Pete loose and gets out of there fast. The saddler jerks the blindfold from Old Pete's eyes.

Old Pete takes an instant to see that everything is clear, jams his head down between his front feet, and lets out an angry bellow. He arches his back and goes straight up in the air, bent like a hairpin. Then he lands on all four feet with a jarring shock. Watching him, you relive the days of the Old West, when this was the usual method of breaking horses.

Needless to say, the guests are not encouraged to take part in this activity. Unless, like the cowboys and the wranglers, you have had plenty of experience, it is a dangerous sport.

Mare nuzzles her foal protectively.

A HORSE OF YOUR OWN

VAN DER MEID-MONKMEYER

So you want a horse of your own? Well, there are a number of things that have to be considered. Besides being a delightful privilege, owning a horse has its responsibilities.

Which One?

One of the first decisions to make is: Which horse is the one for me? Just any horse won't do. You should select him carefully, and you will be fortunate if you have the advice of some older person who knows horses.

The right horse for you depends on many things — your age, your weight, how much riding experience you have had, your general dependability and judgment.

If you're very young, a Shetland pony may be the answer. Ponies are not costly to keep. They are easy to ride, can be stalled and ridden in a small area, and make affectionate pets.

If you are older, however, you need a bigger animal, so that you can take longer rides. The choice here may depend on whether you have a special use in mind. If you want a horse for pleasure riding, he should be gentle, safe, physically sound, and nicely gaited.

How Much Do Looks Count?

Looks, of course, are another thing to consider. Everyone admires a good-looking horse. But to real horsemen, what a horse can and will do is more important than the impression he makes on the eye.

Also, looks are a matter you can do something about. Good food and thorough grooming will put gloss on the coat, spring in the step, and a sparkle in the eye of any horse. By keeping his fetlocks clipped and trimming his mane, you can greatly improve his appearance.

Color, though, is something that can't be changed, so if you have a favorite color or combination of colors, keep it in mind when you choose your horse. Besides the standard colors, there are palominos, pintos, albinos, and showy Appaloosas. These, while not true breeds, are pleasing animals and may appeal to you.

How Important Is Breeding?

Again, horsemen rate the quality of a horse higher than his color, but with modern breeding programs it is possible to have both. For example, a horse may be registered both as an American Saddlebred and a palomino. This means that he has qualified in color as a palomino and in breeding as a Saddlebred. Many of the "color" horses are highly regarded as both pleasure and working horses. They are often featured in the gay parades.

Perhaps the most important thing to consider is your reason for getting a horse in the first place. Is your mind turned toward the show ring? Then a good choice is an American Saddlebred. Would you like the thrill of jumping? Your horse should be the long-legged hunter type. Do you want a showy, dependable, easy-gaited horse? The Tennessee Walker is for you. If you want a horse to win races, get a Thoroughbred. For a rugged all-around working horse, many people recommend a Quarter Horse or a Morgan. Arabians always seem to please their owners.

When you are in the saddle, it is the horse you are riding that counts. But if you are selecting a mount for a special use, get a breed or a physical type of horse that has already proved its ability in the field you are entering.

Morgan colt: Morgans are general favorites for riding and working. Most police horses are Morgans.

How Much Should You Pay?

Another factor likely to influence your selection of a horse is cost. How much can you or your parents afford? Horses may be bought at almost any price, from $50 up. The better ones are much more expensive. Remember that horses cannot be raised cheaply, and it costs as much to keep a poor horse as a good one.

Fine racing, show, and breeding animals bring prices ranging into many thousands of dollars. Pleasure and general-purpose horses are less expensive. Much depends on the locality in which you live, but good saddle horses are often priced around $250. The better ones run two, three, and even four times that amount. As a rule it pays to buy a good one, for horses live a long time, and over the years you will get your money's worth in riding pleasure.

Where Can You Get Your Horse?

This depends to a large extent on where you live. In farming communities and ranching areas, horses are easy to find. Your friends and neighbors may have some to sell.

It is a great advantage to have a chance to examine and try a horse before buying him. Most horses, like most people, have bad habits. They may be given to head tossing, bit chewing, or shying. Though the faults may be minor and completely overweighed by the good features, it is reassuring to know what to expect when you take your first ride.

If you live in a big city, finding a horse will not be as easy, but the situation is far from hopeless. There are the big stables and auctions where horses are always for sale. In buying at such places, it is well to know the dealer's reputation for honesty and fairness, for you won't get much chance to examine and test the horses.

At auctions, horses are brought into the ring and sold to the highest bidder. Some may be bargains, but many are not. Examination is limited, and the descriptions of the individual animals are not always accurate. Often the auctioneer is simply repeating what he has been told to say. This kind of buying is only for people who are quick and capable judges of horses.

Where Will You Keep Your Horse?

Now that you have the horse of your choice, where are you going to keep him? If you have a stable, a paddock and a pasture, you are very lucky. If not, you will have to board your horse, or find a place to keep him where you can give him the care that a pet of yours should have.

It's obvious that owning a horse has its problems, but those who know agree that the fun is well worth the trouble.

Thoroughbreds grazing in Blue Grass country.

KENTUCKY CHAMBER OF COMMERCE

TAKING CARE
OF YOUR HORSE

VAN DER MEID-MONKMEYER

YOU now own your horse. Probably it will be necessary for you to care for him yourself. You'll find that doing this is not only a source of satisfaction, but helps to win his confidence. You do things for him and in turn he does things for you.

Housing Your Horse

To care for your horse properly, you will need a stable. It does not need to be fancy, but it should be clean and dry, and afford protection against extreme cold and heat. Unless your horse is ridden regularly and frequently, he should have an exercise pen or corral. If there is also a small pasture for summer grazing you are indeed lucky, for part of your feeding problem is automatically solved.

'If there is a small pasture for summer grazing, you are indeed lucky."

Feeding Your Horse

The stable should have a feedbox and a hayrack. Normally you will give your horse hay and grain. The hay should be timothy, mixed with alfalfa or clover. Oats are the best grain. Crushed or soaked barley or bran makes a good addition to the regular diet, and your horse will welcome the change.

The amount to feed depends on your horse, his size, appetite, and the work he does. Horses are like people. Some require more food than others. Some will eat too much if they have a chance, and become so fat that they are no pleasure to ride. On occasion, they stuff themselves until they get sick, so keep the oat supply in a locked place. Always measure the amount of grain you feed your horse.

The best guides to correct feeding are experience and the looks of your horse. He should be neither bony nor bulging; his flesh should be firm. Regular small feedings are more beneficial than irregular large ones. Two feedings per day, morning and night, are enough under most circumstances.

Horses drink lots of water, more in hot weather than in cold, and good clean water should always be available. If you have to provide water, this should be done twice daily. Ordinarily horses will drink after eating, particularly if the hay is dusty.

After Exercising Your Horse

This is a good place for a warning. When a horse is hot from being worked or exercised, he should have no grain,

Girls at camp learning how to groom horses.

and only a swallow or two of water until he has cooled out. Eating or drinking at such a time may cause severe stomach cramps.

During the cooling-out period your horse should be led or ridden at a slow walk to avoid stiffening of the muscles. In the case of race horses, the grooms lead them in a circle, with regular pauses at a bucket for a sip of water, until they have completely cooled out. The old saying about walking the first mile out and the last mile back is an excellent one for young riders to remember.

Grooming Your Horse

Grooming — combing, brushing, and rubbing — is a necessary part of the care of your horse. It requires time and energy, but nothing else soothes tired muscles so well or puts such a natural gloss on his coat. Most horses learn to enjoy being groomed and will stand quietly.

A currycomb, a stiff brush, and a rub rag are the tools for good grooming. They are inexpensive, and the best ones are worth the slight extra cost. Some horses' skins are tender, and the grooming must be gentle. Others like brisk brushing, especially on the neck, back, stomach, and around the roots of the tail.

Your horse should be groomed every morning, whether you ride him or not. After he has worked, he should be groomed again. This second grooming is very relaxing, particularly if he has sweated. Sweat brings the dirt to the surface where it can be easily removed with the curry-comb and rub rag.

Caring for His Legs and Feet

Your horse's feet and lower legs should have careful attention, for it is there that lameness is most likely to develop. You can help keep his feet sound by examining them frequently and cleaning out the small stones and debris that collect in the crevices about the frog (the pad in the middle of the sole of his foot). While this can be

"Your horse's feet and lower legs should have careful attention."

done with a screwdriver, a hoof pick does it better and is a good investment.

Shoes should be reset or replaced regularly. This prevents the cramping of the growing hoof and keeps corns from developing. Most horsemen seem to think that shoes should be changed about once every six weeks.

The muscles and tendons in horses' legs undergo great strain during work and exercise. They should be inspected regularly for swelling or heat. Many horsemen habitually rub the lower legs with good liniment during the after-work grooming.

Caring for His Eyes

A horse's eyes should be washed out frequently, particularly if he is being hauled in an open trailer. The membranes and tissues may be irritated by dust and insects, and sore, watering eyes result. Bathing his eyes with a clean rag dipped in borax solution will make your horse healthier and happier.

Keep Him Safe, Clean, and Comfortable

Examine the place where your horse is kept, and remove all nails and loose wire; smooth off sharp corners and cutting edges. The horse can't foresee these dangers; you must do it for him.

The stall is important, too, especially if your horse is in it most of the time. The best flooring is clay laid over gravel and crushed stone. It should be well drained and kept clean. Oat or wheat straw makes the best bedding, and it's up to you to see that it is replaced when it gets dirty. Your horse likes to feel clean, just as you do.

TEACHING
YOUR HORSE

HOBART-MONKMEYER

UNLESS you are an expert horseman, your horse
should already be trained for riding when you get him. No
horse is ever completely trained, however, and there will be
things you can teach him to make him a more delightful
companion and worker. But watch out for bad habits, such
as bolting (making a sudden lunge and running away),
and head tossing, for they are hard to break.

You're in Charge

The first thing you must do is to win your horse's confidence, so that he is relaxed and can give all his attention
to the things you are trying to teach him. If he is nervous
and upset, perhaps expecting a kick or a blow, you can
be sure he is not going to learn much.

Yet your horse must understand fully that you are the
boss. When the horse becomes the boss — and this happens more often than you might think — the situation

The Lippizan horses are world-renowned for their grace, precision, and spirit.

becomes pretty hopeless. Naturally, in such a situation the horse will do what *he* wants rather than what *you* want.

You must respect his greater strength and size, but you should not be afraid of him. If you are, he is not the horse for you. Get a horse that you can trust. In training any animal, your own confidence is of the greatest importance.

Make Him Obey

Obedience is the first mark of a well-trained horse. You must teach him to obey, immediately and completely. Don't let him get away with a half-hearted response — not even once. But remember, it's up to you to be smart enough to know whether or not he is really trying. Never punish him for trying, only for not trying.

Like Teacher, Like Horse

Another thing you can teach your horse is calmness, or "a good disposition." By nature, horses are nervous and sensitive, given to foolish fears. Little things — a piece of paper blow along the ground or a sudden noise — can scare them into a panic.

One of the best ways to develop your horse's disposition is to set him an example of good behavior. Be calm and deliberate when you are with him. Move slowly; talk quietly. Avoid impatience and fits of temper. Don't be upset by the unexpected.

It is well known that dogs resemble their master in temperament. So do horses. It is surprising how much like you your horse will become in a few months.

Always remember that this business of training is a give-and-take affair. If you keep your wits about you, you can often learn more from your horse than he learns from you. And you will be a better rider because of it.

Jumping requires careful training and control for both mount and rider.

JOAN FARBER

A "high-school" horse exhibits the fancy steps he has learned.

RIDING YOUR HORSE

VAN DER MEID-MONKMEYER

IF someone — neighbor, friend, or relative — can give you instructions in riding, so much the better. No one can see himself in action on a horse. You can, however, do much by yourself to improve your riding if you will remember a few rules.

Controlling Your Horse

A horse is controlled by what are called the "aids." The aids are weight, reins, feet, and legs. The art of riding is to use them in such a way that your horse will respond alertly and smoothly.

Fully trained horses become so sensitive that only the lightest pressure is needed. Indeed, the aids may be so adroitly used and so well coordinated that the horse seems to perform without direction from the rider. A horse handled by such a rider is a pleasure to watch.

Appaloosas racing: note the racing positions of the jockeys.

A horse in motion may be divided into two parts, fore and rear. Both must be coordinated for smooth and pleasing action. The reins control the fore part; your feet and legs, the rear.

Using Pressure. Control is matter of pressure, applied in the right places and to the necessary degree. Bit pressure is a signal to halt or slow down. Rein pressure on the right side of the neck will cause a horse to turn his front end to the left. Heel pressure on the right flank will cause the rear part to move to the left.

Making Turns. Turning should be done with the fore or leading part, using the reins. Heel pressure is used to keep the rear part in line. A turn made by the violent swinging of the hind end around is awkward and a sign of improper training or sloppy riding.

Knowing Your Horse

Beginners must learn to use the aids correctly. Instruction will help you understand the reasons for doing certain things. You can also learn much for yourself. Experiment by applying the various aids and carefully observing your horse's reaction. If he does what you want, you can be pretty sure the aids were properly applied.

Since some horses react more readily than others, it's best to start with light pressures. Make them positive and definite, so that the horse will not be confused. Many horses react to the mere tightening of a leg muscle or the slightest shift of the rein hand. You will soon learn the pressure your horse requires.

Remember that control is based on the natural tendency of the horse to move away from pressures. If a trained horse does not react properly, look for possible reasons before blaming him too much. He may have a strained muscle or a stone in his hoof.

Balance Is the Secret

As you continue riding, the proper use of the aids should become an automatic process, performed unconsciously. Yet this is not all there is to riding. If you are to manage your horse capably and enable him to move with ease and efficiency, you must develop balanced coordination.

The horse is carrying an unnatural weight — you and your saddle. If he is to perform to the best of his ability, your weight must always be where it interferes least with his natural action. This shifting and distributing of your weight in time with the horse's movements is balance.

Stunt riding and jumping requires split-second balance and timing.

Balance is a combination of several things. To some extent it comes naturally, but it improves with practice. Lightness and timing are the secret of balance. You should sit lightly in your saddle, your body erect, alert and flexible. Your weight should be distributed through your thighs, knees and feet. Your hands, or hand, should be light on the reins, just giving you the "feel" of your horse's mouth. Your wrists and arms should be relaxed and easy. If you do it right, your horse will be relaxed and easy too.

Timing

Timing is a matter of anticipation, and with experience it becomes automatic. Since you are directing your horse, you should know what he is going to do. So you do it with him, in unison. It is possible to be either ahead of or behind your horse in timing. Both are bad, but being behind is worse and happens much more often. The young rider who endeavors to stay just a shade ahead of his horse will usually be about right.

NOW YOU ARE
IN THE SADDLE

MEERKAMPER-MONKMEYER

NOW you have a horse. He is yours. You know how to take care of him. And you can ride him. But where? When? How?

First, you will have to exercise care and good judgment. A horse is a nonreasoning animal, subject to panic when the unexpected happens. You, as owner and rider, must think for him, must use your brains to avoid situations that might result in serious injury to either or both of you. If you shirk this responsibility, you are not yet ready to be trusted with a horse.

City streets are not good places to ride. Pavement is slippery, and a horse's feet and legs may be injured by the hard surface. Normal motor traffic moves at a speed that is bewildering to horses, and even the best trained animals become nervous. Highways outside cities, unless there is a bridle path well off to one side, are hazardous for the same reason.

Quiet country roads are ideal for riding.

A Good Place to Ride

A good place to ride should have these features: There must be room for the type of riding you plan to do. It must be free of automobile and traffic hazards. The surface should be soft, yet firm enough to give the horse confidence in his action. A few shade trees will add to its attractiveness, while other riders will supply companionship and add to the fun.

Riding in the City

Some cities have riding parks where horses have priority over other traffic, and turf conditions are excellent. Others provide bridle paths where you can ride in safety through pleasant surroundings. Unused ball parks and playgrounds are other possibilities. Fairgrounds usually have tracks and riding areas that are available in the off season. Polo clubs have training and exercise fields.

A determined search of your community is likely to reveal more safe riding places than you believed existed.

Riding in the Country

In smaller towns, riding places are more plentiful. If there is keen interest in riding, a suitable area may already have been developed, and the problem is only one of joining the club. Vacant fields and back roads are generally safe and usable.

In rural sections, it is frequently only necessary to take precautions when crossing the main highways.

On the Western Trails

The luckiest rider of all, however, is the one who lives either in or near the wide-open spaces that still exist in the West. Here there are trails as long and full of adventure as you could wish, with little inconvenience from fences and highways. There is a different trail for every day in the week.

Also, this is the country of exciting pack trips, where one may ride for days and even weeks on U.S. Forest Service trails and never once hear the whine of automobile tires.

There is adventure along the western trails.

The Best Time to Ride

When should you ride? Any time except at night. Horses see well in the dark, but are more easily frightened then. It is especially dangerous to ride on main roads after dark, because motorists cannot easily see horses.

Early morning and late afternoon are pleasant times to ride, particularly in warm weather. There are not so many automobiles moving, and the air is fresh and cool. Your horse will also enjoy the exercise more during these hours. Since he will not get as hot as he does during the heat of the day, the cooling-out and grooming time will be shorter.

Watching Out for Hazards

How should you ride? Always remember that you have a responsibility, both to yourself and to your horse. You must take precautions to avoid being hurt. You must guide your horse in rough, stony going, and protect him from blows, kicks, and cuts. Of course, you intend to do all this, but intending is not enough. You must be constantly on guard against accidents.

Barbed wire is especially hazardous. More horses are injured by barbed wire than anything else. Sedate and sensible horses, when caught in wire, often go crazy and seriously injure themselves in their frantic efforts to get free. The sight of one of those ragged wounds is not easy to forget. Healing requires weeks, even months.

Barbed wire has been used extensively for fences and may be found anywhere. Much old wire is down, lying on the ground or half buried, and this is as dangerous as any. Never ride over it if you can go around.

There is danger, too, in swinging gates and doors. Be careful when taking a horse through them. Injured shoulders or broken hips have resulted from such accidents, and riders have been slammed against these obstructions.

Avoiding Panic

The instinct of a frightened horse is to run, and running horses are the hardest to control. A horse out of control is a menace to himself, his rider, and everyone else in the vicinity.

Always keep your horse under a firm rein. At the first sign of panic or bolting, try to slow him down. If he refuses to stop, use one rein to pull him into a small circle, where he will be forced to reduce his speed. In a small circle most horses soon quiet down.

Creeks and Company

Always take care at creeks and streams. Horses enter water readily, and there isn't much danger at shallow crossings. But in deep water inexperienced horses may become confused and frightened.

Do not ride alone in unsettled areas. It is pleasant to ride in couples or small groups, and safer. Make friends with someone who also likes to ride.

Good Riding!

Going fast is fun. Your horse will enjoy it too, and a reasonable amount of sweating is good for him. But remember that he is a willing and honest creature, and will obey your commands to the point of exhaustion. After a brisk trot or gallop, slow down and give him a breather. Always show him the respect and regard to which a good animal is entitled.

Swing up now . . . and ride!

COURTESY AMERICAN ALBINO HORSE CLUB

DODO KNIGHT